A REMEMBRANCE ANTHOLOGY

I0084903

Footprints on the Heart

*A COLLECTION OF POETRY AND
PROSE INSPIRED BY LOVE AND LOSS*

COMPILED BY
JO-ANNE JOSEPH

Dedication

A thousand days, I've thought about you,
much more than a thousand times,
the memories of you, though few,
are what my heart holds onto.
You live between what was, is and what could
have been,
your absence is felt out loud...

In loving memory of Zia Sarai Joseph
16 July 2013

Blurb

Footprints on the Heart: A Remembrance Anthology
is a collection of Poetry and Prose by bereaved par-
ents from different parts of the world who have been
inspired and profoundly moved by the love and loss
of their babies, which have inspired their moving and
heartfelt words.

They speak of the ugliness, the truth and the depth
of a grief so unfathomable, and the reality of a loss no
parent should have to endure.

Acknowledgements

I want to thank the amazing writers who stood by me through this project. Your words are beautiful and more than adequately reflect what I envisioned this collection to be. I started out by saying that I wanted your submission to be your voice, a way to remember your baby, to have his or her name and memory captured through your words in history and I believe that we have achieved that and so much more.

My hope is that this anthology will find its way into the hands and hearts of many and that they will know a little bit about our precious children as well as find comfort, should they need it, during their own dark times.

You have written with such love and such honestly and I have read each word with reverence, a smile and at times an ache in my chest for what should have been.

Your longing mirroring my own.
Thank you to my husband for standing by me through the
darkest nights and greyest of days. I have had several of those.
There were times when I did not know if I would ever see the
light again. And in those times, I felt your hand on my back and
I heard you when you called me. I love you, I truly do. Losing a
child is something of a mess, isn't it? Losing a wife is a travesty
too, I'm sorry I made you feel that you ever would.

To my son, my shining star, my world. How deeply you love. You
were a constant reminder of what I live for, you are always what
I will live for, you are always my sunshine on a cloudy day.
I want to thank the amazing online community at Glow in the
Woods and my sister across the seas, Mrittika Sen, who found
me when I was afloat at sea one cold night in September 2013.
We float adrift and come together every now and then but we
understand each other in a remarkable way. I hope that we will
meet some day and talk about our traveler and guiding light
over something freshly baked.
I have lived a thousand lives in five years and I am still only
beginning to live this one I call my own.

To our Readers...
I welcome you to take this journey with deep love.

Foreword

Author Jo-Anne Joseph

According to the World Health Organization or "WHO", a Stillbirth is a baby born with no signs of life at, or after 28 weeks' gestation. In 2015 there were 2.6 million stillbirths globally, with more than 7178 deaths a day. The major causes of stillbirth include child birth complications, post-term pregnancy, maternal infections in pregnancy (malaria, syphilis and HIV), maternal disorders, (especially hypertension, obesity and diabetes), fetal growth restriction, congenital abnormalities and almost half of stillbirths happen when the mother is in labor.

The majority of stillbirths are preventable. The statistics are readily available. The experience of stillbirth is a different experience altogether and having experienced the loss of my daughter personally, it is life altering. I have dedicated five years of my life to raising awareness and supporting others through this and I intend to continue working within the community to break the silence.

My story can be summed up simply. I did all there

was to do, leaving nothing to chance. I ate right. I had the best healthcare. I would to this day recommend my obstetrician to friends and family. I never smoked or drank alcohol during those eight months. I went to all my scans and then some when I had concerns, but my baby died of birth asphyxia, a cord accident.

After five years my message is this, grief is a language, albeit an often silent one, but a language nonetheless. It is the language of a mother holding her stillborn daughter in her arms after eight months of pregnancy. It is the inability to cry out, or adequately express the depth of sadness that comes with the loss of a baby. The agony of losing a future and a lifetime of special moments, milestones and memories to be made, with a child who was deeply loved and wanted.

Silent grief is an anguish from the knowledge that society will never completely understand the devastation of such a loss. It is a loss which is often unrecognized and unnoticed, but still very real and significant. It is a loss which is unexplained and unexpected. This is the definition of the grief I felt in those early days after losing my daughter Zia Sarai and in what I still feel now. Yes, the despair has eased over time but it can be described only as learning to cope without a vital limb.

I was deeply saddened at the manner in which people around us reacted in the first few hours and days after my daughter died. There were some acts of sympathy but there was also a myriad of unnecessary comments and advice which we did not need to hear so soon after losing our child. Five years on, I have come to realize that people were probably not sure what to say. Such a loss is shocking and that is understandable; however, I have also come to realize how important it is that people are informed, and made aware of the deep sorrow baby loss parents feel so that they may assist during this very painful journey.

Losing a child in this way is earth shattering. There is no hierarchy in grief. Grief simply is grief. It is very individual and very personal and no-one should have to either defend their loss or have their grief minimized. That said, nobody should go through this alone. We may not completely understand each other's losses but we are required and I dare say wired, as human beings to respect each other's losses, and where possible, offer small amounts of understanding, comfort and support. Because every life matters and as such, every loss matters.

I fell in love with my daughter from the moment I found out she was growing within me, I felt her grow, saw her develop from month to month. A bond was formed and a relationship developed. I began mothering her in those months in much the same way I mother her living brother, my son. And I mother her still. I am the keeper of her memory. I am her storyteller.

Our babies though out of sight are still very much a part of our lives. They are irreplaceable. The significance of each individual life must be honored. If you are a family member or friend of a bereaved parent reading this, you can do this by simply remembering significant days, be it a birthday or death day. Let the bereaved know that they are not alone. The significance of remembrance cannot be emphasized.

Likewise, baby loss parents reading this should offer support to each other and enlighten family and friends in an effort to break the silence surrounding miscarriage, infant and baby loss. People must understand that bereaved parents, although broken in many ways do not need to be fixed. They simply need to know that people acknowledge their babies lives and that they, as parents, have been through the unimaginable.

Above all else, baby loss parents must not minimize their own loss.

Quote

*"There is no greater agony
than bearing an untold story inside you."*

- Maya Angelou

Introduction

How was the concept of **Footprints on the Heart: A Remembrance Anthology** born?

I suppose it started on a cold day in July 2013, when, my daughter, Zia Sarai Joseph, was stillborn. She was just over 33 weeks. She would be five-years-old this year. Zia is one of so many babies gone too soon, yet still loved and deeply missed. I write this introduction on her fifth still birthday. There was no celebration to mark her birthday this year, no flowers arrived, no themed cakes baked in her honor. I can count the number of messages received on hand. But still I am at peace as I freeze my fingers and toes and work on this beautiful collection of words by parents all over the world who have come together to make magic on paper.

Many people have come to know me as Jo-Anne Joseph, the contemporary, suspense and psychological romance author, but I've been writing long before that. I have been writing for the loss community since 2013 in fact, and contribute to several online websites such as **Glow in the Woods, Courageous Mothers and, Still Standing Magazine**. These sites are dedicated to making the journey of baby loss, which I can vouch is often a lonely one, a little less lonely. I have contributed to thought provoking and deeply moving anthologies such as **Our Only Time: A Healing Anthology by Amie Lands**.

I have sat on the idea of a poetry anthology for a while. I often wondered whether I was waiting for the right time to find me, I believe in that kind of thing. Well, this year it found me, a seed was planted in my soul and I knew it was about time I did something to honor and remember my daughter, along with other babies gone too soon through poems and prose.

This is a remembrance collaboration of writers across the globe all coming together to express our thoughts about grief, remembrance, love and loss in words.

What do we have but memories? A box of ashes, a picture in a frame, a few keepsakes. The time we spent with our children was too short, by anyone's terms, but whether they were lost through an early miscarriage, or we carried them for several months or if they lived out of utero for a short while, they lived

They are still with us, intertwined in every facet of our lives. Their tiny footprints across our hearts, their names a valued treasure. This anthology is about remembering who they were and also who we were. It is about marking their names in history, it is about showing the world that they were, that they are.

Love doesn't end when life on this earth does, oh no, love cannot end and so may you find healing in these words.

May our words convey each heart and soul who may not have lived long enough,

But who still lived.

List of Contributors

Kelly Cote

Flora Moore Henneke

Brian Joseph

Jo-Anne Joseph

Michelle Kurtz

Amie Lands

Maureen O' Connell

Stacey Porter

Mrittika Sen

Robynne Knight

The Little Star

BRIAN JOSEPH

Once upon a time, in an astral dimension not very far away, a young galaxy's sun extended his arm to create a place for his future children to live. Out of his bosom flowed the manifestation of love and care in preparation for what he knew would bring meaning to his existence. Milk and honey filled the rivers, stardust filled the air and life filled the land. His preparations were complete. And the land that was created was named Gaia.

He extended his hand again, and as he did, two beautiful astral bodies took their form, shining as bright as he did, with a diamond white sparkle that filled the entire galaxy, and in that moment he knew life would never be the same again, as he saw the entire lifespan of these new stars play out within seconds before him.

He knew the joy and love and life they would bring to this new galaxy.

But as the young stars settled and were about to make contact with the Land to start their journey, a dark shadow from outside the galaxy rose up behind the sight of the Sun or Land, and fell upon one of the young stars. Neither the Sun nor Land knew what was happening, none of this had ever happened before, or so they thought. The darkness engulfed one of the young stars, snuffing out it's light, and the star who at its center was clear crystal, ceasing to burn with that beautiful light, fell to the ground. The Land shook in pain and grew branches of protection around the other young star, the Sun extended his arms as far as he could reach causing a massive bright light to dispel the shadow out of the galaxy. When the darkness left, he turned to what was left of the Litle Star and was unable to mourn for his loss, all his tears burned up in his never-ending flames. But at just the right time, a lone tear made its way out before burning and fell to the ground, to the spot where the burnt out star lay. It embraced her and the Sun's light shone through the tear creating a wave of beautiful colors. The color was so intense, that it caused the crystal to break into a thousand pieces, and as it did, it was flung across the entire galaxy, some of which were thrown into the space above the mother-land Gaia and ignited with the flames from the Sun. And at night, they all glistened, as tiny as they were, in the night sky, reminding the star that survived, that his sister star would always be with him, all around him, in the earth, in the air, in the sky, in him.

And the Sun, Gaia and young star went on to create many more wonders throughout their young galaxy, but whenever they looked up at the glistening little stars, they never forgot their journey here, nor the light this memory brought to them in their darkest hour.

The Story and The Storyteller

MRITTIKA SEN

How will it matter
If I stay awake a little longer?
Tell a story
Wipe a tear
Dig a little deeper
With my little finger?
Whisper, whisper in the darkness
Long words, lost meaning
And yet, a story perfectly formed?
Who should I wake when it's time to tell?
No one watches
The dark daylight with me,
Nor the jagged night.
Only her thought.
Here are only lives lived on snaky streets,
In this cavernous world.
In this cruel, ruthless life,

Here are spoken words, words of vacuous wisdom.

Move. Climb. Buy. Make. Hold.

Here are lives I do not know

And there's a death I know too well.

I make breaths all day

Sitting in the dark.

I never forget to breathe

Or to look back.

To a me I no longer am

And to a girl who no longer is.

Breathe, so you can tell her story.

Breathe, so you can shut them out.

Breathe, so you can walk on with her.

Breathe, so you know she's holding your hand.

Extraordinary life, hers

How can it be penned in the words of the world?

There can be an entire language created for her lips

And a limitless horizon laid out for her eyes.

Clouds can gather in dark skies for her black hair

And her fingers, each the start of a civilization.

There are endless journeys for her feet,

And harvests gathered for her little belly

The histories of this world rolls on the curve of her

shoulders.

She has the sky in her thoughts

She is the earth in her heart,

And she is like no other.

There are roads ahead for this living mother.

All she carries as ration is an extraordinary story at heart.

This is an ordinary life to live

To tell an extraordinary story.

Of how a girl came, and left, on her own terms.

Of how she matched dates with her family's

And entwined her name, eternally,

With her only sibling.

And showed courage and strength.

Of her deep, deep eyes that looked into hearts,

And of all her explorations.

I wake up, yes, I do,

And then I lie awake.

Awash.

A little longer,

A little deeper,

Wrapping my little finger around hers.

I dig deep,

I look wide,

And wait.

For her to wake up in me.

Unfolding the neat curtains of the night,

There's a crack that opens at dawn.
And thus holding her little finger,
I can go within,
To live another day,
A storyteller,
A fellow wanderer,
A traveler,
A mother.

You Are with Us

Costumes, candy, dusk, trick or treaters
We miss you each Halloween
You are not here, but you are with us.

Falling leaves, pumpkin pie, gratitude, family
We're thankful for you at Thanksgiving
You are not here, but you are with us.

Twinkle lights, stockings, peace, joy
We buy a gift in your honor at Christmas
You are not here, but you are with us.

Midnight, resolutions, champagne, kisses
Each New Year another year without you
You are not here, but you are with us.

Hearts, hugs, flowers, chocolate
We share your love on Valentine's Day

You are not here, but you are with us.

Easter Bunny, dyed eggs, baskets, treats
Your name written on eggs at Easter
You are not here, but you are with us.

Fireworks, BBQs, warm nights, freedom
Fourth of July we watch the sky for you
You are not here, but you are with us.

Cupcakes, balloons, cards, nature
The day of your birth we celebrate you
You are not here, but you are with us.

Memories, tears, longing, missing
The day you left, our life was forever altered
You are not here, but you are with us.

Kindergarten, graduation, wedding, babies
All things we imagined you were going to do and be
You are not here, but you are with us.

Winter, Spring, Summer, Fall
Whether a holiday, special day, or every day
You are not here, but will ALWAYS be with us.

Bobby's Eyes

MAUREEN O'CONNELL

Daddy says he remembers your eyes the most,
They were always closed.
So after you died,
we peeked,
We saw,
Blue eyes,
Deepest Blue,
Ocean deep,
Full of secrets yet to be told.

Breathe Carry On

Jo-Anne Joseph

The tears threaten to fall
I wipe them back
breath, carry on
The sadness threatens to engulf me
I hide it behind a smile,
breath, carry on
Anger threatens to consume me
I bite back the words
breath, carry on

I Remember You, Parker

KELLY COTE, PARKER'S MOM

I remember

The joy the moment I found out you were on the way

The excitement of brand new parents-to-be

My first sight of your precious heartbeat as it flickered on the screen

Your little feet kicking me from the inside.

I remember

The moment we found out you were a boy

How you moved and bounced on the ultrasound

The day we picked out your name

Feeling a love, I've never felt before

I remember

How hard I cried when I learned you were sick.

My life crashing down around me

Holding on to hope that you would come home

I remember

Picking out the only stuffed animal we'd ever buy you

Creating as many memories as we could before you

left us

The last kick I would ever feel from you

I remember

The second I heard that your heart stopped

The sounds of your Daddy sobbing

The beautiful double rainbow outside The hospital

I remember

The moment you were still born

How much you looked like your Daddy

The smell and touch of your skin

I remember

How hard it was to say goodbye

The way you made us parents

I remember you, Parker

My sweet angel baby

MICHELLE KURTZ

In memory of Adalynn Kennedy

I think of you constantly and wondrously,
just as the seasons change, so do my thoughts of you.
I think of you every day
I think of you when the snow falls.
Each snowflake that falls on me has me wondering if
that is you saying hello
I think of you in the Spring when everything becomes
new and starts to grow,
You're in each seed that becomes something bigger
and beautiful
I think of you in the heat of the summer,
in each cardinal I see, wondering if you would love the
water as much as we do
I think of you when each leaf begins to fall
and wither in the wind,
and I long to see you in them all

Enough Time

JO-ANNE JOSEPH

I'll give you a minute,
The doctor's words ring in my ear.
A minute to sort through the daze,
A minute to take in that the baby was gone,
A minute to cry out in pain.
We'll let you spend some time with your family,
The nurses consider me sadly,
An hour or two to talk about nothing,
and everything,
Mourning the loss in our varied ways
Mourning the loss of the child
Mourning the loss of mind, heart and soul.
Time to go to the delivery room.
To deliver the baby,
An hour more and the baby arrived,
without a sound.
Minutes to hold her in private

Minutes to hold the sleeping child for the first time
I could no longer ignore she wasn't alive
A minute to realize she wouldn't cry,
Two more hours and then Goodbye.
Time to go to the funeral.
Time to drive home with a tiny bag of ashes.
You just need to eat and sleep a little,
Family fussed about,
You'll feel better in the morning.
Six weeks of leave from work
Drinking in the absence and emptiness
Aimless, powerless
Waiting for the madness to subside.
It didn't.
Years have passed.
I still see the looks of concern
Crossing faces every now and then
Not voiced, but there,
It's not healthy that she's still sad
It's so sad she doesn't want to have more children
Is this writing about the baby really helping her?
I see it and say nothing.
I don't need to.
They think I've had enough time.

Are You There?

JO-ANNE JOSEPH

Maybe you're there in the stars
looking down at me
as I search for you
Maybe you line them up in a certain way
just so I know you're with me
I feel you in the breeze that surrounds me
in vastness of the night sky above me
as endless as it is,
as is my love for you dear one,
I gather my arms around me,
I take in a deep breath,
I let a tear fall,
as I whisper your name...
Are you there?
Do you hear me?

Mother Earth in the Springtime

MRITTIKA SEN

April is the cruelest month, breeding
Lilacs out of the dead land, mixing
Memory and desire, stirring
Dull roots with spring rain

The Wasteland, T. S. Eliot

It's never just the sun, rising in an azure sky with
birth-like promises. Never just the lilacs, breeding
from a forgetful land that pretends it never knew
what it is to die. Never just the spring rain,
drenching the hopeful world with newborn showers.

It's never just... Anything.
Always something more.
Or less.

It is cruel, dull, dead, this is Spring for me.
This April, my daughter's birth month. The cruelest
month.

* * *

They named me Mrittika. My poet father, upon the
urging of his sister, gave me a "meaningful" name
when I was ten. My aunt thought that Gypsy – my
formal name until then – was too informal, and
would never be taken seriously when I grew up. So,
at ten, I went from being a traveler to one grounded
to her roots.

Mrittika. Soil, Earth, Mother Earth. In Sanskrit, the
ancient language of undivided India, the language of
the sages, the yogis, the evolved. As Mrittika I grew
up into a young woman, found my foothold, my
place, defined, refined, redefined. I lost it, found it,
and lost it again. Lost it more, lost it high in intellect,
lost it sure, lost it deep in love. Then as Mrittika, I
plunged into my soul to plant the saplings I could
spring from my core. I found him, then her, in that
depth.

It was Spring. After a ruthless, brutal, toiling Winter,

trees were blooming. The bulbs colored as my belly swelled. Then on a spring dawn, alone in bed, the ocean surged in me. My little explorer Raahi, who moved like the waves inside me, washed me ashore. I was alone with her big brother that morning, waiting for her father to come home in the evening from a distant city, when she decided to take me on a voyage with her. The voyage of her birth. Of the explorer landing on earth. Reaching her, and my, destination. I was alone when I drove my three-year-old to pre-school and drove myself – five hours into labor – to the hospital. I felt the ocean in me. I felt the earth in me. I was the earth.

I was Mrittika again. Soil, Earth, Mother Earth, baring my heart, baring my flower in Spring. She sprung from my womb, pink and full of life. She sprung out, like a fountain throwing life high into the skies, sprinkling life far and wide, from the depths of the roots I thought my fears had dug. She sprung out, her arms stretched at the sun, her face glowing at me, her mother, her earth. I became Mrittika again. Mother Earth in Spring.

Then she died. In the heat of Summer, on a night

that thunder roared, she withered, and quietly drooped into an everlasting sleep. The nurse at the ER scooped me from the floor, now a pile of useless dirt, slipping through her gloved fingers like quicksand. She looked down at those uncontrollable trickles, and said that my little flower has now entered my heart. There, she said, she will live from now on, growing roots into her permanent home. Permanent? Home?! I asked her, "She's really dead? She's really dead? She's in my heart? Where in my heart? Where is my heart?" In that heart I lost that summer, Raahi would now apparently reside. It was not a place she would spring from, bloom in, flutter, toddle, walk, run to, from, in, around. It was where she would, as they say, rest in peace. A baby. Resting. In peace. Just the irony of those words could shake and shatter the earth into rubble. And it did.

She had a white box, and a dress, all too big, blue with white flowers, and a lime green border. It had been our favorite summer dress for her. She had white tights, versatile and useful in summer, that I had carefully chosen for many of her colorful dresses. She had my wedding ring, the one with the infinite union on it. She had two blades of grass, from her birthplace, still green after four days in a car. She had my life, the love her father and I shared, the beauty and wonder of our firstborn, her big brother. She had our hearts. She had it all. In nothing.

They sent her down, down into the earth's womb. The earth, Mother Earth, her breast bared, her arms stretched, knots of twisted roots covering her head, her eyes looking into the horizon, into my dead eyes, took in my baby.

I became Mrittika again. Soil, the Ground, the Earth. Mother Earth, in whose hollow heart a baby's broken shell now lies in a white box. I am Mrittika now. More than I ever was. A bare, barren earth, even, especially, in spring.

I became meaningful. As I became meaningless.

* * *

Now the trees are alive again. There is once more the green of life. The leaves are back.

The colors of life are spreading far and wide, the music of the fresh wafting in the air. Again, once again, here, everywhere, the voice of the new, the words told a million times, and yet whispered for the first time, every spring. New. New. New. Alive. Alive. A-l-I-v-e. The land, young again, swaying, laughing, like a newborn. The sun is warm, golden, newly washed. The earth is rejoicing in its birth, in the circle of life. The dance of life continues in circles around me.

It was not like this, you know. Soon after she died, the trees died too. One by one, they shed their leaves, their flowers curled up, their shadows grew longer. The soil dried up, the sun mellowed, the air grew languid and heavy. The earth seemed to reach a breaking point. As if it grieved, as if it sunk to the hole in me. Tired, rusted, broken, it sat in it with me for a while.

Then it rose up, and covered itself in a white shroud. White, the color of death, when it has devoured all colors of life. The trees stood still, like ancient souls, in submission, in resignation, as if there will be no tomorrow. The sun gleamed a cold light, the earth filled with snow. The sky lightened, the air sharpened. The earth was peaceful, empty, white. As if it grieved, as if it showed the emptiness in my heart to all, when I could not.

***

It is spring again. Three relentless years of spring. It never stops. It a-l-w-a-y-s comes back, like a stubborn plague poisoning my blood, unsure if it accidentally spared some drops the last time. The same spring, proclaiming, pretending, to be freshly squeezed and new every year.

Life is back on earth. My baby is not back. She was born in spring, three years ago. She is still dead in this one. She came to me with the return of life, her newness filling my soul, her birth giving me, her mother, her earth, my last, only, meaning. As life is returned to this earth, she is not returned to me. I become Demeter, calling after my Persephone. I become the wasteland, breeding lilacs from the dead ground, trying to mix my few memories with a lifetime of desire.

Nothing brings her back. The mythical daughter returns to her goddess mother, if only for a few months. The human one doesn't. New poets write new lines celebrating, bemoaning, cursing, championing, spring. I feel the same sting on my face, like a million tiny daggers digging a million holes into the earth's broken surface, from which nothing springs.

Life continues. Despite death. Death continues.
Despite life.

Time

JO-ANNE JOSEPH

The years have passed quickly,
time after all is a slave to no man,
let time pass, I say bravely,
it will not diminish my love for you,
I feel your absence like the skin ripped off my body,
I feel it like an ache in my bones and muscles after a
long day,
it eases and returns,
eases and returns,
there were days when I was crippled by sadness,
days when I was drowning in madness,
I reached for anything that could steady me,
I fell several times and got up again, wobbly,
but I realized that the unsteadiness I felt wasn't
foolishness,
the only foolishness was in denying the absence I had
grown accustomed to,

I am a crippled happy fool now,
I smile and I laugh because I live in harmony with the
pain,
The pain is real,
The joy too,
It is as real as I am,
I cannot exist without either.

Holding Bobby

MAUREEN O'CONELL

Through all of my tears,
I remember thinking
Holding you was a good birthday present.
That day the hospital staff finally let me hold you
happened to be my 34th birthday.
It had been over thirty hours since your birth and I
finally got to hold you.
My God, you were beautiful, a perfect bundle in my
arms, 6lbs 6oz of Pure Love.
You couldn't open your eyes or kick or cry but you
could Love, Love, Love, Love, Love.
I am your mommy. You are my baby. We share a love
beyond time and space.
Four years after your death and I feel you – you are
strong.

Alone

She often sits alone
barely understood...

Parker,
I Hope You Know

Kelly Cote, Parker's Mom

I hope you know how much I love you and that I
think of you each day.
I hope that you are proud of me and proud that I'm
your Mom
I hope you know you have touched so many lives and
continue to live on through us
I hope you know we wanted you and that we'll never
forget you.
I hope you know that you will always be a part of our
family
Above all, I hope you feel loved and wanted.

The Day She Died

JO-ANNE JOSEPH

The day she died,
I shattered into tiny fragments too small for the eye
to see,
Even if I searched my whole life, I would never be
able to find the pieces.
Some were swept up by the wind and scattered
across the earth,
some melted into the sea and some,
some simply disappeared.

The day she died, I felt an ache in my heart.
It intensified day by day month by month, and year
by year it grew stronger.
The ache was crippling and I curled up in a ball of
hurt from which there was no escape.
No amount of medication could ease the hurt.
I feel it still, in my heart, where she lives.

The day she died, I got stuck.
The wind came and blew all around me, but I
couldn't move.
The rain pelted down around me, soaking my hair
and clothing but I was a prisoner.
This was my four by four, this place inside my mind.

The day she died, I cried soundlessly and then vigor-
ously.
It was a cry that haunted my dreams, not the kind
that could be heard throughout the land, this was
a forever cry, the tears of the soul as it weeps and
suffers regret at its naivety.

The day she died, I gave up on the illusion of a happi-
ly ever after.
It was like being awakened from a deep sleep, where
the light dawns on you and you feel lighter for shed-
ding that burden of untruth.

The day she died, I shed my beliefs.
I let go of false pretenses and religious teachings.
I looked in the mirror and reminded myself that I was
human.

We are human.

This is it, all we have right now.

I was not going to waste another day thinking other-
wise.

I removed the shackles that bound me and I set
myself free.

The day she died, I said goodbye to the old me who
laughed about everything, and had hope in the un-
known.

I realized I was wearing a mask, and let it fall, and
along with it my ideologies about the way things
should be.

The way I should be.

The day she died, I unplanned.

I stopped waiting for the right time because there is
no such thing.

The right time is now.

I let go of lists and just went with it, figuring I'd get
where I needed to be in due time.

The day she died, a future was destroyed.

There would be no stories to tell, no myth or magic.

All those should have been and could have been are

hidden in these stories, our stories, and her story.

The day she died, I lost my daughter, my little girl, my
princess.
I lost my light, the one that burned brightly at the
thought of my hopes and dreams for her.
All I'd worked for, all I'd hoped to be to her.

The day she died, my soul bled.
It still drips inside of me.
The crimson liquid seeps into every part of me, a
reminder of what I've lost.
What I'll never be able to fix.

Letters to My Heart

FLORA HENNEKE

Dear Camille,

My sweet angel, it is difficult to put into words what I
want to say. It's been a week since your heart stopped
and the day my heart broke in half.
You are my first born.
The daughter I always wanted. The daughter I
longed for.

Sweet Camille
I do not know why God chose you to be an angel.
But I do know you are the prettiest angel in heaven.
I don't feel much baby.
I am very numb and I cry a lot.
I finally took down your nursery and that about
killed me.
I had to put your beautiful teddy bear blanket I was

supposed to wrap you in into a box.

I had to store your butterfly swing in the closet.

How is that fair for any mother?

I remember the sweet jumper I wanted to bring you home in, and the big pretty pink bow. The white and pink socks. My favorite onesie was pink and white and said "Texas Longhorns".

Momma is a big Longhorn and Steeler fan.

Camille, I do know that we will be reunited one day.

I will never feel your hugs here in this lifetime, so I have to settle for the wind on my face.

I will never see the sparkle in your smile or the shine in your eyes so I have to settle for the sun and stars.

No words in the English language can describe my pain.

I would not wish this pain on my worst enemy.

No parent should ever have to live without their baby.

Waking up without you here every day feels like I am just living.

I don't feel the joys of celebrating your birthday, Christmas' or first day of school and all the many other firsts without you.

All I can do is wonder what every year with you would have been like.

Would you be a princess girl or a camo girl?
These are things I can only guess baby girl.

How is this fair?

A mother and child belong together.
I want you to know I fought for you.
I did all I could but I guess God had other plans.
Just please know Camille, you are forever loved and
never will be forgotten.
My heart will forever have a hole that only you can
fill.

A mother's love never stops.
Just know as long as I live, your legacy will live in my
heart forever.
I can't explain why this happened when it did.
There were just two weeks until your delivery.
No it's not fair, and I wish everyday baby girl that it
didn't happen this way.
Not to Us. Not to You.
Camille I don't know if you remember,
I used to sing Jesus Loves Me to you, while I carried
you in my tummy.
I have been listening to that song lately, and I have to

trust that Jesus knew what he was doing, because I
have no answers.

Love,
Mommy

The Little Things

JO-ANNE JOSEPH

Sometimes it's the simplest of things,
The way the wind feels against my skin
The way the cold seeps into my bones
Sometimes it's the absence of the warmth
The sound of my boot soles on the floor as I walk
Sometimes it's a sound,
The rustle of dry leaves on the ground or a song
A sad song...lyrics unimportant
Just the melody
The weight of the melancholy I carry with me
Just those simple things remind me
of time lost
Of a life that ceased.
Of you.

Searching for Bobby

Maureen O'Connell

In my dreams

I got to keep you and heal you with my Love.

But when I woke up, you were gone

So I keep searching and

I have found

Traces of you

In your brothers at play

The sky on a clear night

Rays of sun

The chirping of birds

The changing of seasons...

...The strand of pearls my mother gave me was lost

for months and your older brother found it in my

winter boot...

...I like to think in some way

we will be reunited.

The Absence

JO-ANNE JOSEPH

Suddenly, when the baby died,
the body found itself on its own
The organs functioned optimally to get it to do what
it needed to, but the soul had vacated.
The body went through the motions. It held the
baby, cried, and ate, slept and cried some more.
The body picked out the clothes the baby should
wear and read through the baby's journal.
The body attended the funeral, during which she sat
silently wondering where the soul had gone to,
missing that part of itself, wanting it to come back.
But deep down the body enjoyed the desolateness,
it was proof that the baby had been taken from it.
There was blankness behind its eyes that hadn't been
there before.
There was a numbness that wouldn't go away.
The body wondered if it were to drive a knife

through it, would it bleed.

To bleed was to feel and the body felt nothing.

Still some months later, the body roamed the darkened house late at night, often reaching for a second bottle of wine, hoping that if it was filled with oblivion, maybe the soul would return to it.

Oh but the body was weak, the pain crushed it and bruised it.

Often the body wondered if it would survive another day without its companion and friend, old soul.

The body became afraid that it would never again have that connection.

All the while the soul searched, it searched for the baby everywhere, it flew through the cracks and crevices, and it called out for the baby.

Come back.

The soul couldn't go back to the body, just yet—it needed answers, needed to find where the baby went and ask her to come back with it.

That would heal the body, wouldn't it? For the body had rejected the soul, that moment when the doctor said the baby had died.

The body pushed the soul away.

The body was cruel, heartless, refusing to let the soul back in.

Surely if the baby was found, all would be well again.
The body wouldn't be so still anymore.
Surely.

On Your Still Birthday Parker

KELLY COTE, PARKER'S MOM

On your birthday, I should be spoiling you with
presents.
Instead, I cry thinking about what could have been.
I pull out all your pictures and the few mementos I
have.
I cry.
I remember every detail from the moment I found
out I was pregnant to the moment we said goodbye
at the hospital.
Replaying all of it.
Partially to make sure I never forget. After all these
are the only memories I have of you, if they fade they
will be gone forever.

On your birthday I should be lighting a candle on a
cake, instead I light one on the mantle.
I should be throwing a party for all your friends.

Instead, I place a party hat on your urn to show you that your birthday matters, too.

On your birthday, I'm reminded that it's been another 365 days without you.
On your birthday, I remember you, honor you, and continue to love you, just as I do all of the other 364 days in the year.

Letters to my Heart

FLORA HENNEKE

Dear Camille,

As you can see my life will never be the same without
you here with me,

My heart will always be split in two.

I wish there was more I could do.

One day we will be reunited,

until then, I will live for you.

As long as the sun shines in the sky,

As long as the birds fly high,

I LOVE YOU.

As long as the moon shines in the dark,

As long as the stars' shine in the park,

I LOVE YOU.

As long as the rivers run deep,

As long as the mountains are steep,

I LOVE YOU.

As long as the trees are tall,

As long as the clouds don't fall,

I LOVE YOU.

As long as fish swim deep,

As long as frogs continue to leap,

I LOVE YOU.

I LOVE YOU, Camille, and I always will.

Love,

Mommy

You Are There

JO-ANNE JOSEPH

You are there in the sunrise
As the light emerges on the horizon
Your colors spread across the sky
You are there at the start of each new day
I acknowledge you as I open my eyes
As my breathing normalizes
I smell you in the fresh air
Feel you in its crispness
You, my dear child,
Are in all things beautiful!

Of Love

Brian Joseph

What shall I say of you oh love?
Are you the sweet kiss of the morning dew?
Or the first rays of the healing sun, awakening me
from the deep.
Are you the sweet smell of roses in the Spring time?
The sparrow's first song with whom my heart does
sing.
The feeling of the grass under my feet on my moun-
tain top
The smell of home after a long adventure?
Or the feeling of safety after being lost for eternity?
And yet I cannot afford you all these honours, oh
love.
For within my canvas of breath-taking colour,
There is a darkness that threatens to engulf me,
Until all my colour is swallowed up in your abyss,
And the fires of hell call to me.

How can something so beautiful be so sinister at the
same time?
And then I realise, oh love,
You are both a blessing and a curse,
The light and the darkness,
A force of nature,
neither asked for, nor which one can live without,
to ensure survival, until your task is complete, and
then, like a betrayal you leave,
And the longing for you once more remains,
Only never to be filled again,
Empty,
Hollow,
still longing...

*(Originally published work by Brian Joseph in the novel
Infinity by Jo-Anne Joseph)*

July

JO-ANNE JOSEPH

I don't want June to end,

I don't want to have to fight July again fight and lose,

hopelessly,

dismally,

I don't want to have to face yet another death month,

cold, heartless death month,

I don't want to feel it creep up on me yearly,

stripping my skin off my bones leaving me standing

completely, utterly bare,

July

the month of uninvited tears,

the month of deep sorrow,

you, heartless bitch of a month,

how I hate you!

There should be a way to erase you,

wipe you off the calendar in one clean swipe,

shred you to pieces and leave you bleeding on the

floor,

you callous month of dread,

I despise you so,

Bring me September,

Bring me Spring,

Bring me December,

Oh let me snuggle my toes in the sand and breathe in the sea air,

Let me not experience July again...

I count the days as it approaches

10, 9, 8 now 7...

you're at my doorstep,

surely I can choose to leave you out there,

6, 5, 4 now 3...

where the cold can shred you bare,

where my daughterless-ness can die along with you.

Bobby's Wisdom

MAUREEN O'CONNELL

The mind and spirit are not the same.
My second son taught me this.
My greatest teacher,
He suffered a traumatic brain injury in utero (a cord
accident).
Doctors told us when we take him off the machines,
His brain will stop telling his lungs to breathe, his
heart to beat.
Though he had very limited physical abilities,
His presence was strong – his spirit so sweet and
Loving.
I am so touched and forever changed and so proud of
him
For his incredible beauty, for all he suffered and gave.

The Progressiveness of Time

JO-ANNE JOSEPH

Time is progressive, it moves forward constantly,
increasing the infinite space between then and now.
It cannot be slowed down, paused or completely
halted.

Time has a past but it is forever in the present or
future, so in essence time somewhat diminishes what
used to be with what is and what will be. Time urges
one to take a step forward, no matter the direction,
just forward, onward, on.

Seconds to minutes, minutes to hours, hours to days,
days to weeks, weeks to months, months to years,
such is the fault in time, it cannot be stilled.

Time lost cannot be recreated, you cannot decide to
rewind time, it just doesn't work like that. It never
did nor ever will. Much like words spoken cannot
be unspoken, deeds done can't be undone, and time
diminished cannot be retrieved.

Time as it progresses distances me from my past more and more every day, I am further away from anything and everything I have ever cherished in days passed. I am moving further away from where I used to be, often unwillingly, yet I keep moving, such is the fault in time. I have no control of time. It cannot be contained. Time is a master to itself. Time forsaken cannot be used again, time wasted is lost, and time never looks back.

Seconds to minutes, minutes to hours, hours to days, days to weeks, weeks to months, months to years, such is the fault in time, it cannot be stilled.

Another 365-day Journey without you

JO-ANNE JOSEPH

Every day, the distance between then and now grows

and I grow older

but she doesn't

Every day, I stand at the cusp of yet another day

I take yet another step into tomorrow

and she sinks further into history

Every day, I wake up and I am reminded

of a life I can only ever dream of,

a life which she should be a part of

Every day I whisper I love you to the wind

I imagine she is somewhere there to hear it

but she doesn't say I love you back

So I will never know

I begin yet another 365-day journey around the sun

without her

More memories in which she doesn't feature

This is all the life I have so I will live it

Every day, I will live it as best I can
I will fight just a little bit
because she is always here with me,
out of sight, but in my heart.

Candle Light

JO-ANNE JOSEPH

in memory of Jadene Joseph

I watch the flickering flame,
As it dances in the evening light,
And I marvel at its luster and warmth.
This flame though small, illuminates the whole room,
And in so doing, illumes my heart
In this flame there's a steady promise
Of the love we shared over the years
And the love we share still
And in that memory
I feel the warmth return,
It flows through my heart and soul
And I now see the light shining like a tiny beacon of
hope
This candle burns as a symbol of that love and hope
It's where I find you,
It's where you live forever

Letters to my Heart

Flora Henneke

Dearest Camille,

My Baby girl,
Although, I never had a choice in losing you, I chose
to live for you every day and make you proud.
When you left this world, a part of me left with you.
Mommy is as happy as I can be, as hard as it is that
you're not here.
Although I am no longer with your Daddy, please
know it was not your fault.
He did not know how to love other people, and I
wanted better for you and me.
I wish you could have met my husband today.
He doesn't just love me;
He loves you too!
He has two children that I love as much as I love you,
and they love you too!

All three of them help me keep your memory alive
which means the world to me.

I wish things were different every day, baby girl, and
you were here with me.

I fought for you hard, bargaining and begging.

But, God had a bigger plan that even 7 years later I
still don't understand.

I know you are pain free and no longer sick, but you
are still my child and I should be able to care for you,
not live without you. I look at the photos from my
wedding and I cry.

I wish you were there.

Two families becoming one.

It shouldn't just be a picture of you on a memory
table.

You should have had a beautiful dress on, with
flowers in your hair, standing next to me at the altar.

You should be here playing with my husband's
two children, not lying six feet under the cold hard
ground.

I should have memories with you, not just the eight
and a half months when I carried you.

You are my world Camille.

Did you know you are named after the strongest
women I know?

They were fighters and I know you would be too.

God just had his own ultimate plan for all of us.

I still yell, scream, cry and ask WHY? WHY? WHY?

I believe seven years later I deserve some kind of
answer as to why my baby died.

I did nothing wrong.

Yes, I know you were sick with a heart problem but
that's where the specialist and doctors came in.

Why didn't I get a chance to be a real mommy?

Although, I read that heaven is a nice place, pain free
and no tears, how is this fair for me?

If only I could have you all the time.

I guess I can't argue that the Lord is the best
babysitter until we are reunited forevermore in glory.

Love,

Mommy

Words

Jo-Anne Joseph

Words are where I found you again,
When I thought I'd lost you,
Words led me to you,
Like a beacon through the darkness,
When I write I can see you,
I can feel you,
I can hold your hand and share my heart,
In this world of Words, you never truly leave me,
You grow as my story does,
We share things we never will in person,
In my lonely hours, when I miss you most, words
comfort me,
Words have been my healing,
The balm to my aching soul.
Words have been my refuge.
It is where we will always meet,
Words bind us together forever.

The Wish List

JO-ANNE JOSEPH

Every day I wish for you,

An endless string of repeated wishes which will

never come true,

I wish for the strength to hold the tears at bay,

or the honor of being called your mother to be

known,

for the world to understand that I will never stop

wishing,

never stop wanting,

Always,

every day,

Forever....

Symbols

MRITTIKA SEN

It is a box really, if you ask me.
Nailed on four sides, it could be a coffin,
Except I cannot lie dead in one.
Too real. And not true.
Instead, I live, dead, stuck in a box
Breathing sixteen millimeters of stale, dark air.
Some days it feels like a trap,
A tricky contraption, carefully designed
To stifle me, slowly, painfully,
And yes, alive.
Other days, it stands empty like a junction,
A stop sign, where I paused,
Before my life took a very wrong turn.

If you ask me for symbols, imageries, similes,
The metaphoric, the literal,
I will indulge you.

With a half-smile, an elusive gaze,
(That make me look like an evolved,
Esoteric being, lost in thought)
I will tell you what grief looks like,
Tastes, smells, sounds like.
Wait, I can even let you touch it.
I only touch it rarely,
But when I do, I scratch it, peel it
Little by little,
With my middle finger.
If you want to touch it politely though,
Please do. I think you'd like that.
Ugliness is not grief's twin word
Until it touches you back.

And then, when you've come close, you think,
I will tell you about the time,
The exact time, date and all,
When grief felt like a bed.
Oh, of roses, you think?
(We're talking in metaphors after all)
I don't really remember that detail.
So you're free to imagine.
I can just tell you how I lay in it.
Floating like air, daring to feel comfortable,

Until the bed started folding.

It wrapped me, engulfed me,
And folded my skin shut.
It gathered layer upon layer of me,
As I flattened in peace.
Yes, I know, I was folding into pieces too.
But I remember the peace more.
So I think you should know
That grief can be peaceful too.
I folded up, neat, quiet,
Shrinking, wrinkling every minute.
And yet, I still breathed the
Sixteen millimeters of stale air.

You can tell me to look for the keys,
Out of the box,
Or make a more carefully-designed plan
To escape the trap.
Surely I can look for directions
To find my way back
From that one wrong turn?
You don't quite grasp the image of the bed.
(It's too vague anyways)
So you think I should focus

On the other symbols.
Try to make sense, find a way,
Come to terms, look for answers.
Take the symbols for real,
The metaphorical for the literal.
Maybe art therapy would help?
To draw out my grief.
So it's not too drawn out.

I think you could be right. Or not.
Or somewhere in between.
(As we all apparently are, you think)
But would you mind if I said,
That my strongest symbols are words?
The way I meaninglessly string them together.
In circles, squares, pointed towers,
Stacking them up until a ball of silence
Drops into the cacophony.
The words fill the shapes,
Stretching them at the seams,
They're strung, stacked, cracked,
Each running ahead of the other,
Each breathless with the emptiness
Between itself and what came before.
You see, I never find the one that follows.

What, who, should have followed me,
Didn't.
So now every word is a spinning atom,
A bounded square box,
A wrong turn, a purposeful trap,
A betraying bed.

So, as I think, speak, write,
My bereaved life in unbelieved words,
I scatter them around like bubbles,
I shatter them apart like glass.
And through a wall of welling water,
(No, not my tears, silly!)
I look for her face,
And my pieces in them.

Love

JO-ANNE JOSEPH

I am not always sad at the thought of you,
sometimes I remember you and I smile.
Genuinely smile,
and I wonder about what would have been.
When I think of how much I love you, there is joy in
that,
because you are a constant reminder that love is so
much more than what we see.
Love is so much more than what we can say to each
other every day.
Love is even more than we can possibly do.
Loving you has been my great lesson in love.
I say that with deep passion and truth. It's true, you
were loved long before I saw or touched you,
but the great truth is that when you left you did not
take any of it away, it still remains,
in my heart, in my soul, in everything that I am and

ever will be.

It is there when I glance at the picture of you from a 4d scan done just a month before you died.

"How can you love a child you do not know?" one may ask, "a child you have never heard, talked to or spent a day with?" I answer simply, "You can".

You can.

Every child is woven carefully and eloquently into the very tapestry of a mother.

They are within our hearts, our blood, our cells, they are within our very being. There can be no mother without a child nor a child without a mother, we are from one another and of one another and we exist in that way. Not a corporeal child, a child, a child for which you prayed for, a child for which you hoped for, a child you dreamt of, a child whom you love, a child whom you carried, no matter how short that time or how long. You see love is what knits our souls together Zia, it's what will always be the proof of your existence, the proof of your significance and the evidence that I will love you forever.

It still hurts but I can breathe

JO-ANNE JOSEPH

I savor the sweetness of the smell of my son's hair
and skin
It still hurts but I can smile
I sit outside and soak up the sunshine like I used to
It still hurts but I can walk
I hold out my hand and caress the petals of the roses
blooming in my front garden
It still hurts but I can sing
I listen intently to the chirping of the birds in the
trees
It still hurts but I can dream
I lift my eyes to the sky and see the blue again
It still hurts but I can hope
I look to the sunset in the evenings and whisper I
love you to the wind
It still hurts but I can live
I open my heart and let grace in

It still hurts but I can share
I hold hands with another and let love in
It still hurts but I can love.

The Mother of Sadness

JO-ANNE JOSEPH

She carries sadness in her arms
Cradles it against her chest
Nurtures it with tears and heartache
The mother of sadness is she
She whispers to sadness in her darkest hour
She calls to it in her deepest need
Sadness engulfs her
Sadness overwhelms her
The mother of sadness is me

My Heartbeat

Jo-Anne Joseph

My daughter died

One cold day in winter,

She drifted off into an endless sleep

She struggled for a day, maybe two,

Trying to unwind herself from the cord

As it tightened its hold around her,

and all the while I never knew

She tried to get free

And when all was lost,

I have to believe

She tried to hold on to the only sound she knew,

My Heartbeat

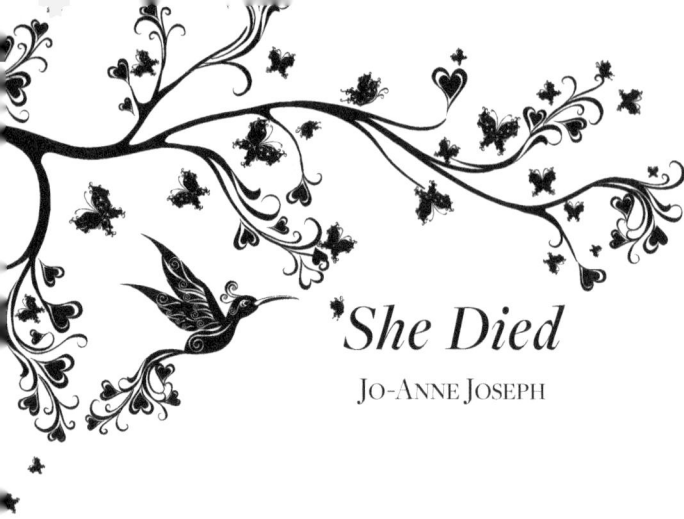

She Died

Jo-Anne Joseph

She died in the only home she knew,

I met her sleeping,

and never heard her cry,

I never felt her fingers wrap around mine,

And now I search for her in the stars above me,

I call out to her in my dreams,

I stare at the sunset and imagine her staring back at

me,

My daughter died world!

And she took a part of me with her

A part of me that was always hers,

She died, yes,

But more importantly she lived

The Flower Child

JO-ANNE JOSEPH

Yellow petals in her hair,
Yellow roses, gypsophila circles her crown,
The flower child,
Her yellow dress sways slightly in the wind,
The breeze catches her curls
Her laughter an eternal song,
My soul longs to hear.

Letters to my Heart

FLORA HENNEKE

Dear Camille,

I wish I could tuck you in tonight.
A mother has the right to tuck all her children into
bed.
How can I live with all this anger and jealousy?
Is it fair for me to watch a TV mom lose her baby,
bringing back every emotion in tidal waves?
Is it fair that I hear certain sounds and it brings the
tears and hurt in torrents.
Is it fair to live trapped like this?
Is it fair for me to see everyone else have healthy
babies when mine died?
Don't get me wrong, I am truly happy for them, but,
it's more a sense of jealousy because I want you,
Camille, and no one will ever replace you.
I can't answer all these questions, no, it is not fair.

Growing up I was told that life is not fair but I never imagined that meant that I had to give up my daughter and live without her.

Then I also have to live with the guilt of how low I got after you died?

I turned to alcohol, drugs, binge eating, and I even wanted to end it all, just so I could be with you.

Is it right for someone to go through all this and also be looked at as a failure as a mother?

People cruelly label you as a statistic or a murderer if they don't know what happened.

No! It is not fair! And seven years later it does not get easier and the pain never goes away.

Some days I cannot function and I don't even want to be around people. Other days it's ok but I still have to fight the anxiety.

Is it fair that I had to go through almost six years of therapy for the anger and the depression and the drinking? No!

My anger was so bad baby girl, I would black out and would not know what I was doing.

I blamed everybody and everything for your death, even God!

That's right, God!

Can you believe it baby? The mommy that would

sing Jesus Loves Me to you while you were in my tummy turned her back on God when your heart stopped.

I prayed continuously for you to be healed and healthy and I received nothing. I was also told once that it was my sin that killed you.

If that was the case, I didn't want any part of Christianity. I constantly asked myself why a God that rose Lazarus from the dead, who performed many more miracles, who defied death himself, could not save an innocent baby?

I questioned everything in the Bible. Was it real?

Did it happen?

What's the point in trusting God?

Does He hear our prayers?

I stopped going to church.

I stopped fellowshipping with friends.

I stopped singing.

I slept for most of the day.

I stayed at home not welcoming company. I was in my own world searching for answers for several years. During this time, I continued to drink heavily and my anger grew stronger. I was forced to move back to my parents' house. Now an added humiliation, I was twenty-two years old living in my parents' house with no job, no kids, no school and nothing to offer.

Suicidal thoughts and fighting with my parents became a frequent thing. I just wanted it all to stop. How is it fair to put a young mother through all this? Then one weekend I was invited by a family friend to a church concert at the church I used to attend. At first I refused but my mother encouraged me to go and have a good time.

I eventually decided to go and it turned out to be very a very emotional and heartwarming experience. I cried all night and I believe, at every song. There was a testimony that night and I learned that I was not the only one who had ever lost a baby. I learned that what I was feeling was normal. I learned that I was not alone. When I got home and as the days went by the anger though still there began to dissipate. I began to read the Bible again slowly. Although it did not bring you back it did start helping.

Eventually I was back in church singing and fellowshipping and enrolled in school for my C.N.A license. I graduated in 2014 and got a full time job right after graduation.

In January 2011, I lost your great grandmother. Losing both you and your great grandmother were hard for me to bear but somehow I got through it with God's saving grace.

I learned through all this that I am human. I make mistakes. I am not perfect and not supposed to be nor am I supposed to paint a pretty picture of your death.

The Lord was always right there to help lead me back and pick me back up. Camille, I am telling you this because I want you to know that I didn't just move on or that I intended to make losing a baby look easy, as some people have told me.

That is definitely not the case.

I want you to know I had to fight and still fight every day to get my life back on track and to what is my new normal.

As I lay here tonight I just hope you are proud of how far I have come. I work and fight every day to keep the anger and anxiety away with God in my life. Like I would have taught you. I miss you more than anything. Remember how I told you before, that you were named after some strong women, well you were named after YOUR MOMMA and your great grandma. How cool is that? The biggest fighters of all. I don't quit and I am stubborn. I will continue to fight for you my baby bear. With the Lord on my side

and knowing one day we will be reunited forever-
more is my motivation. I love you sweet girl.

Love,
Mommy

The Flower Child

JO-ANNE JOSEPH

Her bare feet on the earth
Her arms outstretched towards the sunlight
The light dances in her eyes
My flower child
The sunflower, the orchid
The daisies in full bloom
My flower child
Precious flower child
My world needs you
I treasure the memory of you
I hold it dear
Every month we spent together
Every minute I held you in my arms
Every day I felt your movements
Every scan I now value so much
I treasure the day I saw you
When I held you for the very first time

How you fit perfectly into my arms
The feel of you
My lips against your cheeks
Your lips
Your temple
I hold dear those precious moments
It's everything I will ever have
I remember your face
Your tiny hands and feet
Your soft hair
Pink lips
Every part of you is so special to me
I have no pictures to remind me
I simply treasure it all

The Question

JO-ANNE JOSEPH

It plagues me,

A shadow over me wherever I go,

It chases me constantly,

Incessantly,

Vicious in its pursuit,

It is a constant reminder,

Of my loss,

Of my incapability,

Of my inadequacy,

The Question comes at me unpredictably,

It is always unpredictable,

a knife in my back,

a thorn in my side,

It is an ever present memento,

Of her absence,

Of my deep longing,

Of my deep regret,

The Question,
It follows me all my days,
It weighs me down,
It engulfs me,
The Question plagues me,
It shadows me wherever I go.

Remembered

Jo-Anne Joseph

Each little soul so loved and wanted,
each little heart stopped beating so soon,
each little life so deeply treasured,
each little presence though absent, still measured,
each little face so beautifully crafted,
each little form so preciously unique,
each of our lives so completely altered,
by each little heart we so loved and so wanted.

Push and Pull

Jo-Anne Joseph

Every day I feel myself moving one day further away
from you,
but a day closer to you too,
I feel the emptiness of your absence consume me,
I feel too the deep love I hold for you urging me on,
Every day I feel restless about the missing link in our
chain,
but I feel stronger too,
that I am able to stand,
as hard as it is sometimes,
Every day I am grateful for the time we shared to-
gether,
for the conversations only you and I were a part of,
Every day I forget a little,
but I remember too,
Every day I conjure up images of your little face,
though it has somehow blurred,

it is there,

always there,

Every day, precious child I miss you,

every day I am caught up in the loss of you,

Still, every day I cherish the fact that you were,

and always that you are.

Letters to my Heart

Flora Henneke

Dear Camille

I have been doing a lot of thinking about my
birthday lately.

I will be almost 30, and I should have a bouncy 7
years old baby girl.
Instead I have to go to your grave, as I do every year.

Where is the book that says this is fair? My wish
every year is to have one more day with you,
to hold and kiss your sweet face and hold your little
body once more.
Where is it written that a woman shall be punished
this way for eternity?

The worst punishment of all is what comes afterwards.

The awkward looks, the "so called friends" stop com-
ing around and stop calling, the whispers, the family
that doesn't know what to say or do so they don't
invite you to things or the worse they just say "shake
it off, you can have another kid".

I am still human, I am still me, I am still a person with
a heart, mind and feelings that needs support like the
next person. Just because I am able to have another
child will not replace the one I lost.

Is it so selfish to want what belongs to me?

Baby girl, this is one topic I have no answers to, but I
sure wish I did because I do have plenty of questions.

Why my daughter?

Why me?

What did I do?

What did she do?

How is this fair?

How am I supposed to go on knowing my precious
daughter is six feet under?

Who decided this was ok to torture moms like this?

When will the pain stop?

In a month I will be blowing my candles out and all
I will wish for is to hold you again and not just your
blanket.

Sweet heart please know I am never mad at you.
Like I always say, I am mad at the situation.
I just want you with me more than anything in the
world and I would give up anything if it would bring
you back.
I love you sweet heart.

Shine bright for mommy.
Love Mommy

The Cracked Jar

JO-ANNE JOSEPH

The jar which was once full is now cracked in the
most awkward places,
It doesn't really matter what is put in or at what rate,
it simply drizzles out seconds later.
It stains the table cloth it is placed on and the beauti-
ful mahogany table beneath it,
The jar is Unquestionably and most evidently flawed,
It is no longer a sight for the eye to behold,
instead it lies on the mantelpiece mostly untouched,
Its character altered and its destiny unknown,
The jar is now cracked in the most awkward places.
That jar is me.
It can hold only as much as the crack will allow and
that to for a time unknown.

Of Hope

BRIAN JOSEPH

What shall I say of Thee, dear Hope?
Are you the setting sun in my life, or a shining star in
my sky?

I remember thee in my childhood,
How you came to me when I was afraid and alone,
Making me trust in friendship again...
How you came to me when I doubted myself,
Making me rise to the opportunities before me,
Then, when I lost faith in childish love ...
You made me believe again.

Yes, how childish actions and needs also require your
soothing...

And yet I stand at the edge of nowhere seeking you
once more.

My needs not childish, my aching not small.
Will you soothe my soul the way it needs?
Or will you break my trust as you did before?

Oh Hope, my friend, my illusion...
Canst thou save me once more?
Should I rise to your hand...
Wilt thou protect me this time?

(Originally published work by Brian Joseph in the novel
Destiny by Jo-Anne Joseph)

Letters to my Heart

FLORA HENNEKE

Dear Camille,

I carried you for eight and a half months before your
heart stopped.

You are mine.

My sweet September baby.

I was thinking yesterday how hard things really are.

Is it fair that I want to hide away during the months
of September, October, November and December?

Is it fair that I really do not like social functions any-
more?

Is it fair I have to go through the torture of people
asking questions and having to relive every moment
or be pitied?

What do I say when people ask me how many kids I
have?

I always say three, but it gets uncomfortable when

they ask to see pictures of you.

What am I supposed to do then?

Where is the handbook for losing a child?

They have thousands and thousands of parenting
and birthing books, but what about a book on what
to do when your baby dies?

Since I don't have pictures of you, and I don't like
the awkwardness of telling people I lost a baby, that
forces me to lie. I say things like, "Oh, she was run-
ning from the camera," or "she was not at home that
weekend,"

Does this make me a bad person?

Does it make me a bad Christian?

Does it make me a bad mom?

I don't like being pitied or just being labeled a statis-
tic.

I'd much rather talk about you like you are still alive
than put myself through the alternative.

Maybe one day I will be at a place where I can tell
people I have three children but the third one died,
but right now, it's "I have three children," - period.

Talking about you like that helps me keep your mem-
ory alive and makes me feel like you're still a part of
our family.

I scream and cry some days when I see family photos

because I know they will always be incomplete.
Just know baby I am never mad at you.
I am always furious at the situation. That will never
go away whether I accept your death or not.
I have to live my life with this pain and it is time to
embrace the reality,
"I'M THE MOM OF AN ANGEL AND PROUD OF
IT!"

Love,
Mommy

Forever Home

Jo-Anne Joseph

I was broken when you left me
Hollowed out,
Cold
I felt tarnished
But I have come to see
That there is value in me
It took me a while
But now it's clear
You knew only me
Only my love
Only my warmth
Only my heartbeat
For that I am sacred
I am so much more than I thought
I am forever your home
Still,
I am missing so much of myself without you
I will never be whole

Hollow

JO-ANNE JOSEPH

The world came tumbling down around me,
the impact of it I feel in my soul,
there is only darkness, there is only confusion,
no matter where I turn, I am desolate,
I am hanging now by a thread of uncertainty,
shadows no longer walk alongside me, they threaten
to devour me,
the weight of it all is overwhelming,
the questions are endless, it's too much to bear
I turn to the light but it is no longer there,
it has disappeared,
I've realized what it's like to be abandoned.

Try Again

JO-ANNE JOSEPH

Brutal words,
It implies that before doesn't matter anymore,

it implies that I must move forward,

it implies that I must count my losses,

it implies that she was a gamble,

she could have stayed but had to go,

it implies that I didn't try hard enough,

it implies that she didn't matter,

it implies that she can be replaced,

it implies that I have failed.

If Only

JO-ANNE JOSEPH

If you had asked for my heart,

I would have given it to you,

Without a thought,

Without a doubt,

It would have been yours,

It would have beat for you,

It would have lived for you,

If only you had asked,

I would've gone to the moon and back,

I would've,

If only...

Together

JO-ANNE JOSEPH

I loved you every second of your life
I will love you every second of mine
Your heart beats and mine are forever entwined
Your soul became a part of my own
I was your only home, your sacred place,
An honor I proudly hold
You're no longer with me
But you've woven your way into me
There you'll be
Forever with me
The light that'll never fade.

Gone

Jo-Anne Joseph

My new life has you in it but I can't see you,

It is a life of experience,

one of anguish,

A life of scars that run deeper than the eye can see,

My new life is one of endless tears,

Then there are times when there are no tears too,

the numbing dreadfulness of it all,

My new life has you in it,

it always will,

but it's one of yearning for you,

it is full of aching arms,

an aching heart,

a torn soul,

My new eyes cannot see girl babies, without feeling

sick,

My new eyes cannot block out the dreadful screams

of newborns,

It's my life,
My life with and without you.

Zoë Remembered

ROBYNNE KNIGHT

One night near the end of my pregnancy, I woke
up to the odd sensation of Zoë hiccuping inside my
belly.

It was such a strange feeling - impossible to describe,
but one my friends had told me I would feel.

I can't explain the incredible sweetness

and undeniable sense of "there is another human
being inside me" that came over me in that moment.

I put my hand to my belly, overflowing

with love, and felt Zoë's heel slide past my palm as
she kicked her little legs.

It was the first time in my pregnancy that I had felt
an actual body part I recognized.

It was unmistakable.

I know some women can tell their baby's

head from their bottom, and their elbow from their ear while they're womb-side,

But it all just felt like unidentifiable curves to me.

Until that moment.

Her tiny heel.

Her tiny hiccups.

I wish I had been able to feel those same movements after she was born,

to let her kick her feet against my palms

and soothe her little hiccups.

But I am so grateful for those fleeting moments we had together.

I will never forget them.

Orange Lilies

STACEY PORTER

Delilah Evangeline, every mother I speak to who has
lost a child has found a little something that reminds
them of their lost little one.

Every. Single. One.

For me, this reminder is the orange lily.

It is vibrant, and breathtakingly beautiful, and deli-
cate, just like you.

But they also hold deeper meaning.

See, lilies are not uncommon, and once the bud has
opened, they don't stay in bloom long.

Like preemies, each has grown in different soil, under
different sunlight and with different sustenance.

Each story is their own.

I've always thought that as part of an arrangement,
lilies accentuate, yet they also demand the eye's focus.

You, my lovely, are the same way.

You add to the beauty of our family, and our hearts

always, but you also provide something more pro-
found.

In the spring and summer, it's always comforting
when I come across a little reminder, at a street cor-
ner, at the park, or in someone's front yard.
In winter, the days are dark and it's sometimes hard
to breathe.
My oxygen seems stifled.
But this is the pattern of mother nature, so I keep
going.
You have taught me that demanding attention to
the needs of hurting mothers, who take on so much
often at their own expense is critical.
Supporting them through the season after season of
sunshine, rain, drought, and blizzards is one of the
most meaningful things I can do in this lifetime.
You have also helped me see that there is a lot being
asked of our mamas, and they are not being cared for,
so they sometimes become just as delicate as the lily,
and sometimes they fall apart too.
It's really bittersweet - because of you, I've been able
to understand more than I ever thought possible
about grief and loss, but also resilience and strength.
There are times when it's exhausting to tend the

flowers, but because of you, I know I've been able to help plant these seeds for other hurting mothers. Because you were with us, I have learned more than I ever thought possible about a lot of things. I've never really had a green thumb, but you have allowed me to become a florist, and to flourish myself.

In fact, you've inspired me to start a nursery of my own, because for me, your influence is everywhere, and that stays with us longer than any perennial ever could.

When we meet again

JO-ANNE JOSEPH

when and if we meet again,

will you know me?

will you pass me by, smile, nod or stop,

will you hold my gaze for just a second?

will you hold out your hand to me in welcome,

will you greet me, Zia?

will you thank me or disregard me?

honor me or not even remember me at all?

will you hold me, when we meet again?

or will I you?

will you change much or completely?

will I recognize you, will you me?

will each moment I've lived without you seem end-

less

or will it not count at all,

will I be healed entirely?

will those holes in my soul be filled, mended, covered?

will my heart be made whole again?

will we meet by daylight or by night?

will it matter,

will I see more clearly?

will I finally know?

will you love your name and ask me about it?

about why I named you light,

or will you already know, and smile knowingly,

will you lead me into a happiness I could not experi-
ence,

here in this place that doesn't have you in it,

will you touch my face, wipe my tears?

Pry the whiskey from my palms,

will I cry at all?

when we meet again Zia,

will it be the end?

or the beginning of something greater.

About the Contributors

JO-ANNE JOSEPH

Jo-Anne Joseph is an independently published contemporary romance, suspense and psychological thriller author. Along with a passion for writing, she is an avid reader and enjoys painting and coloring. She has a deep love for poetry and prose. Her lifelong love affair with words started at a young age and resulted in her release of five full length novels, a novella, as well contributing to two anthologies. Jo-Anne is a business professional by day and also writes on a volunteer basis for on-line publication Still Standing Magazine and websites Glow in the

Woods and Courageous Mothers. Her articles have been republished in several newsletters.

Jo-Anne lives in Johannesburg South Africa and is happily married to her husband Brian for eleven years, they have two children, Braydon who is a little scientist at just nine years old and baby Zia who lives in their hearts.

"I lost her body. All that remains are held in a wooden box in my home. I find her every time I share her story or reach out to another soul shattered by loss. I bare my soul willingly."

www.joannejosephauthor.com
info@joannejosephauthor.com

* * *

MAUREEN O' CONNELL

Maureen teaches high school and middle school Art in Northern Idaho. She is the mother of three sons: Hugo, Bobby, and Finn. Painting, dancing, and camping are among her favorite activities.

* * *

Amie Lands

Amie is a wife, mother, teacher, and author of Navigating the Unknown and Our Only Time. She is the proud founder of The Ruthie Lou Foundation and a Certified Grief Recovery Specialist®. Her most sacred role in life is being "mama" to 3 beautiful children: her daughter, who she held for 33 days, and her two sons who she has the privilege to watch grow. When Amie learned that her daughter would not survive, writing became her emotional outlet, used as a way to process her emotions and to educate others on the grieving process. Through grief work, soul searching and heart healing, joy has found its way into Amie's life once again. This has become her passion and calling: to write, to educate, to advocate and to offer hope for bereaved families. Amie's work can be found at www.amielandsauthor.com

* * *

Mrittika Sen

Mrittika Sen is a wife and mother to two beautiful children. She received a PhD from Northwestern University's Department of Communication Studies in 2017.

"Raahi was my dream come true. She was everything I ever imagined in a daughter, and much more. She was the restoration of my faith in my life, the completion of my family, the one to take us on a spectacular journey. After twelve grueling weeks at the NICU and two surgeries, she came home healthy and happy. Eight days later, she wandered on, alone, leaving the three of us to only trace her path. As we imagine all the time, what it would be like to walk with her, we live every day knowing what it is to not be able to. I try to walk with her in bringing up her big brother Aahir, whose hands she holds forever, and whose life and name she will eternally be entwined with. Together, they are AAHIRAAHIRAAHIRAAHIR. A perfect equation, a never-ending poem, my children. I walk with them through my writing, and I am Raahi's Mom."

* * *

ROBYNNE KNIGHT

Robynne Knight is a writer, educator, acupuncturist, and mother to her beautiful daughter, Zoë Amara, who was stillborn on July 25, 2011. After a healthy, full-term pregnancy, Zoë was born still into her mother's arms after a traumatic labor and birth, with no official cause of death identified. This experience changed Robynne forever, as she was forced to carry the greatest love alongside the most intense grief she had ever experienced.

Along the way, she has learned to find beauty in the present moment, growth and healing in the depths of grief and loss, and gratitude for the connection and support of others who have experienced grief and trauma. Robynne started The Zoë Project in 2012, donating teddy bears to bereaved parents in maternity wards, and offering supportive resources and information to families who have experienced neonatal loss. She is a contributing writer and content editor at Still Standing magazine. She is passionate about helping others, and loves traveling, spending time in nature, writing, and practicing yoga.

* * *

Brian Joseph

Brian Joseph lives in Johannesburg South Africa with

his wife Jo-Anne Joseph and son Braydon. Losing their daughter, Zia Sarai, in 2013 is what brought them to the baby-loss community.

"For me, I personally felt silly and even guilty for feeling sad about losing my child, we are brought up in a society and time that rarely recognizes this as a valid loss, and is only now coming out of the shadows with subjects such as losing a baby. Many people are confused as to why a baby whom we never knew for a long time could mean so much or have such an impact on the lives she touched. I am grateful for this community being available to those who need it and to be able to share our story along with others who understand our hearts."

* * *

Flora Henneke

Flora is a wife to her soul mate and best friend, Matthew. She is a mom to 3 beautiful children. Becca, who is full of southern sass and class, is a typical preteen. David is a typical boy who loves trucks and tools and keeps her on her toes. Last but not least, there is Camille, who Flora holds in her heart forever. She was her stillborn angel and forever, her baby girl.

After losing Camille, she kept a journal from day 1 and it has been her escape from the pain.

Flora lives in South Texas and loves to spend time with her family, cooking and baking. She also enjoys volunteering at her church and spending time with friends and family.

* * *

STACEY PORTER

Stacey has been dedicated to supporting families who have suffered infant loss and traumatic birth since 2013. She is founder of the Tangerine Owl Project, an Illinois nonprofit devoted to offering peer support to these families, started in memory of her daughter after a NICU loss in 2012. Stacey is also heavily involved in both local and national organizations which support maternal mental health, as it intertwines so greatly with pregnancy and postpartum experiences for mamas.

* * *

MICHELLE KURTZ

Michelle Kurtz is a devoted wife to her best friend
Marlen and mother to 22-year-old Brittnie,18-year-
old Kameron and angel baby Adalyn Kennedy in
2015.
Michelle has a deep desire to help others with their
own grief and loss.